QUILTING LESSONS

Kara Gibson

Ellen Curtis

QUILTING LESSONS

Ellen Curtis and Karen Gibson

REDEMPTION PRESS

Published by Redemption Press, PO Box 427, Enumclaw, WA 98022

Toll free 1-844-2REDEEM (273-3336)

Redemption Press is honored to present this title in partnership with the authors. The views expressed or implied in this work are those of the authors. Redemption Press provides our imprint seal representing design excellence, creative content, and high quality production.

Quilt Block Credits:
All traditional quilt blocks featured in *Quilting Lessons* are in public domain:
Broken Dishes and Pinwheel quilt, 2003, by Laurie Ensign, Kirkland, Washington; see page 14.
Dove in the Window block, 2017, by Shannon Bennett, Duvall, Washington; see page 26.
"Hope: The Seed of Life," 2011; quilted by Joni Petrica and stippled by Nancy Calar-Hardy, Vancouver, B.C., Canada; block pattern by www.quilterscache.com; cover photo.
Ohio Star block, 2017, by Shannon Bennett, Duvall, Washington; see page 86.
Tumbling Blocks quilt remnant, c. 1932, North Dakota; Betsch family heirloom; see page 106.
All other featured quilt blocks, c. 2011-2013, by Priscilla Cook Gibson, Bellevue, Washington.

Photo Credits:
Front Cover: Quilt in wooden chair by Peggy Olafson Curtis, Mill Creek, Washington.
Back Cover: Ellen Curtis photo by Sheila Flickinger; Karen Gibson photo by Alicia McAskill.
All photographs of featured traditional quilt blocks by Peggy Olafson Curtis, Mill Creek, Washington; www.peggyphoto.com.

ISBN 13: 978-1-68314-459-5 (Paperback)
978-1-68314-460-1 (Hard Cover)
978-1-68314-461-8 (ePub)
978-1-68314-462-5 (MOBI)

Library of Congress Catalog Card Number: 2017951954

In memory of my father, Cliff Curtis (1928-2014), our beloved Connecticut Yankee. Your love and loyalty to family, your generosity, brilliance, wisdom, and perseverance inspire me. Remembering your advice and listening ear still encourage me.

Ellen Curtis

Donald, you are my other heart. I love and respect you more today than when we first married. I am so thankful and grateful that the One True God is intertwining our hearts together in Him. As we travel along the pathway of life, you are a rich blessing to me. Thank you for your constant support, belief, and encouragement and for filling our home with your music.

James, you are the child we thought would never be. You are the precious tool God is using in my life to shape and mold me into the image of His Lovely Son—Jesus. I love you more than I can express and am so glad that God let me be your mom. You are a constant joy and delight.

Karen Gibson

ACKNOWLEDGMENTS

We are thrilled to be holding a copy of *Quilting Lessons* in our hands. It's been quite a journey to get here! We have spent hours writing and praying together. Just envisioning how this book might bless and encourage you kept us going.

We would like to acknowledge and thank Redemption Press for bringing this project to publication. Athena Dean Holtz and her team have been outstanding to work with.

The inspiration for the quilt stories and meditations lies in the traditional quilt blocks. We'd like to honor Priscilla Cook Gibson (1927-2014) for creating the majority of the blocks specifically for this book. Her love for family and passion for quilting will always be remembered.

We would like to thank Peggy Olafson Curtis for the beautiful photos that adorn this book. When we first dreamed about this project years ago, we'd only hoped for full color! It is a delight to see the quilt blocks captured through her artistry.

We recognize that this devotional has been brought to life because of our families and friends. They never stopped believing in this project. Their support and confidence has meant the world to us!

We are praying that the Lord brings blessing, healing, and a deeper experience of His love for you as you read *Quilting Lessons*.

Ellen Curtis and Karen Gibson

INTRODUCTION

Any quilter knows that perfection is elusive as she sews dozens of pieces of fabric into an intricate design. Even with expert stitching to bring it all together, little imperfections become apparent. Our 30 traditional quilt blocks are no exception. Elegant photographs reveal tiny and charming flaws. Just like our lives, the featured quilt blocks have minor mistakes and misaligned points.

One of the beauties of a quilt is that once all the blocks are stitched together, their deficiencies are no longer noticed. We, too, need the assistance of a Master Quilter who sees the overarching design, purpose, and beauty of our lives. However, in our own eyes, we tend to scrutinize defects rather than see the big picture.

In a similar vein, as writers, we strive to make our words as clear and vivid as possible. We struggle over word choice, polish and edit sentences, striving for a cohesive message. After our manuscript is complete, we may find that there are still small blemishes.

Whether we are quilters or writers, our amazing God takes our mismatched points and our frailties and incorporates them in a masterful way to show His grace.

We submit to you the timeless lessons we've learned from these quilt blocks. Enjoy the blocks' color and charm, knowing that we are all a little like them. In the hands of our Creator God, we can become something quite lovely!

CONTENTS

2

ALBUM

Philippians 2:3-5—*Do nothing out of selfish ambition or vain conceit. Rather, in humility value others above yourselves, not looking to your own interests but each of you to the interests of the others. In your relationships with one another, have the same mindset as Christ Jesus.*

On top of my antique washstand is a collection of family mementos, including old photos, a china thimble, a lone teacup, and a delicate vase. Among these treasures is a worn leather guest book which belonged to my great-grandmother, Josephine Carpenter. The faded entries written in the 1880s to "Josie," as she was known to friends, hint of the love and faith they shared. Cora wrote, "Josie, may I ever be a bright stripe in your rag carpet." Another friend encouraged her, "May your chief thought ever be your individual responsibility to God."

Visitors from Ohio and Kansas reveal clues that my great-grandmother was kind and hospitable. Her sister Stella penned, "I shall always remember my visit at your western home with much pleasure." Another well-wisher promised, "With much love I remain your friend." These simple greetings written over a century ago whisper of a woman's loving life that greatly influenced her family and friends.

Reading Josie's guest album reminds me of my special friends and the many memories and hours we've shared. Like the popular Album quilt, with each of its blocks lovingly stitched and signed by a friend, I can point to people who've had great influence in my life.

One who has made a lasting impact is Kathy. We grew up sharing Barbie dolls and playing hide-and-seek. As a teen, she shared with me the life-changing news that I could have a relationship with Jesus Christ. Over 40 years later, Kathy and I are still dear friends and life-long sisters in our faith.

Relationships are like the Album quilt's colorful blocks. Each acquaintance is like a new quilt patch, presenting an opportunity to add our signature of love and hope. We choose the colors and the stitches. Are we adding something of value to our family and friends' lives? What clues about our priorities do we reveal to those around us?

A family album, an heirloom quilt, or a single teacup may be left behind, but the faith and love that we stitch daily into the hearts of those we influence will outlast all the treasures of our lives.

My Prayer

Lord, help me to be like You and see the needs of others before my own. May I be sincere and loving and leave a lasting impression. Help me choose the colors and the stitches that will leave behind the hope and promise of Your never-ending love. Please let me be a "bright stripe" in the rag carpet called Life—living each day fully for You!

My Response

My attitude should be the same as that of Christ Jesus.

ANVIL

2 Thessalonians 3:5—*May the Lord direct your hearts into God's love and Christ's perseverance.*

Stepping from the bright sunlight into the dusky blacksmith shop of a recreated pioneer village, I stood to one side of the doorway while I waited for my eyes to adjust to the dim light. I heard the rhythmic clanging of metal and the whooshing sound of bellows used to fan the flames. I felt the fire's warmth from where I stood. As my vision cleared, I noticed the blacksmith's tools. Tongs used for grasping hot metal and hammers pounded the iron into shape. A large steel anvil stood in front of me; nearby, a tub of water used for cooling the material rested on the ground.

The blacksmith drew a piece of red-hot iron from the fire with tongs. Placing it upon the anvil, he pounded the metal. When it cooled, he thrust it back into the fire, where the heat softened the material, making it easier to mold. He repeated this process until the heated object was pounded into the desired shape. Because the block was made of a different substance, it left its imprint upon the piece being fashioned. Satisfied, the smithy plunged the piece into the water to cool before beginning the finishing touches.

I left the shop and wandered the streets of the village. I thought about the men and women who lived during our country's pioneering days. No farm would be without the anvil or the skills of a blacksmith. His craft was necessary to fashion horseshoes, wagon rims, and barrel hoops. He also repaired farm tools and created nails. Given the anvil's importance in everyday life, it is not surprising that pioneer women chose to design a quilt block pattern focusing on that tool. The popular depiction uses a striking combination of light- and dark-colored squares and triangles to make up the Anvil patch.

Like the smithy's metalworking, Jesus Christ uses the stresses and trials of life to mold us into His likeness. He permits us to be tested by fire through difficult times so we become pliable in His hands. Jesus uses His Word as a tool to shape and reveal where changes in our life or attitude are needed.

When we endure the pounding and shaping process on the anvil of life, we develop qualities such as perseverance. As Jesus places us on the anvil, His loving imprint is left upon our hearts. We are crafted into a valuable instrument for service in the Kingdom of God.

My Prayer

Jesus, I often resist the fire in which You place me. Help me to endure the pounding process of the anvil, instead of resenting it. I desire to see it as Your craftsmanship and that You want to leave Your impression on my heart. I want to become a true reflection of You. Help me be willing to be fashioned into a useful tool and show Your loving attitude in all the circumstances of my life.

My Response

May the Lord direct my heart.

BIRDS IN THE AIR

James 1:25—But whoever looks intently into the perfect law that gives freedom, and continues in it—not forgetting what they have heard, but doing it—they will be blessed in what they do.

The rustling in the cattails ended as a pair of red-winged blackbirds darted out, their scarlet patches visible as they took flight. Pausing on my morning walk along the shores of Lake Washington, a solitary Great Blue Heron watched me as he stood regally among the tall reeds. I held my breath, realizing I was catching a rare glimpse of him at dawn. Overhead, a flock of Canadian geese flew gracefully in formation. The air felt crisp and cool, signaling summer's end. How do the birds know to begin their journey south each year? Instinctively, they find their way to warmer climes, only to return and renew the cycle of life in the spring. Taking a rest on the dock at Marsh Park,

I sat entranced as the sunlight shimmered on the lake's surface, creating hundreds of silver sequins. I marveled at the beauty around me and how nature obeys the rhythms of the passing seasons.

The blackbirds, herons, and geese appear to be free. Like all birds they follow their instincts to fly south or north, to mate, and to rise at dawn and sing. They follow the laws that have been set down for them and are free to be exactly what they were created to be. In the Birds in the Air quilt, the patterns of triangles seem to fly in formation across the quilt top. Its intricate pattern did not just happen but was creatively pieced by a designer. We can recognize the artist behind the quilt—and in nature.

When we give our hearts over to the Creator God who orders nature, we can find that liberty we long for. Within the loving boundaries of His spiritual laws we can find release from fear, guilt, and shame. When we walk with Him, He gives us the ability to become who we were meant to be. As we realize and accept our purpose we find a measure of satisfaction, freedom, and beauty in our lives. Like the birds, which heed God's natural laws, as we align ourselves with Him, we find deliverance and peace.

My Prayer

*God, I want to experience the release You promise in Jesus Christ.
I don't want to let my problems hold me back from seeing You at work
in my life. Like a flock of birds in flight, I want to obey Your ways and
be free. Please, let my heart climb upward on the currents of
Your love and soar.*

My Response

As I look intently into the perfect law that gives freedom,
I will be blessed in what I do!

14

BROKEN DISHES

2 Corinthians 5:17—*Therefore, if anyone is in Christ, the new creation has come: The old has gone, the new is here!*

Looking forward to high tea, we stopped at Queen Mary's, a popular British tearoom at the edge of Seattle's University District. A portion of one wall is inlaid with broken teacups and saucers, all creatively refashioned into a mosaic, a crazy quilt of colors and florals. While waiting for a table, we wondered about the stories behind the broken dishes. Could the fragment of the Royal Albert cup have been a first piece of china collected by newlyweds? Maybe the chip of Blue Willow was part of a cherished service that someone's aunt used each time she entertained guests. While we chatted, the hostess called us to our table and we ordered our tea.

Perhaps the naming of the Broken Dishes quilt represents that universal need to remember broken things. The women who designed the quilt block may have remembered their beloved treasures left behind on a move out West. For many, their precious dishes—and dreams of home, family, and security—were broken along the way. What secrets were held in those quilts? Maybe quiet offerings of broken dreams, countless prayers, and tears were stitched into the triangle-shaped, four-patch pattern.

Broken dishes, broken dreams. Our hearts long for safety, home, family, and for everything to "stay put." We agonize for loved ones to recover from illness. We're crushed when a career ends with a sudden layoff. Friends, children or spouses fail us.

Broken dishes, broken dreams. What do we do with ours? Are they swept up and bitterly tossed out, yet the memories linger in our hearts? Are they offered to God as a sacrifice, with a willingness to see what He might do with the shards? He can be trusted with broken things. He has promised that in Christ we are a new creation. He makes beauty from ashes. He turns mourning into joy.

Could our broken dreams and disappointments be an offering to God? He patiently waits for us to lay them at His feet. Just as women have treasured the family ragbag for what the fabric scraps could produce, the remnants of our dreams are God's treasured construction material. With them safely in His hands, He freely begins the gentle repair and reconstruction of our hearts.

My Prayer

O God, I give you the shattered pieces of my life. You alone can take them and make them into a beautiful mosaic. I can't make sense of how the pieces should fit together, but You have promised in the Bible that You understand the pattern for my life. You allowed Your perfect Son to become broken and bruised for my sake. Thank You for helping me find my way to You.

My Response

The old has passed away, the new has come!

CATHEDRAL WINDOW

Psalm 43:3—*Send me your light and your faithful care, let them lead me; let them bring me to your holy mountain, to the place where you dwell.*

Sitting with my sister Becky at Le Mont-Saint-Michel, we watched the sun create wavy patterns on the stone walls and uneven floors of the abbey. Falling under the spell of the stillness and peace of the monastery, our eyes followed the graceful curves of the high-arched windows filled with dozens of diamond panes. Some were gray or light blue, but none of them clear. Looking through the panes, the images on the other side appeared to be drawn with blurry, smudged lines. While the opaque, thick glass let in the light, it distorted the gardens outside.

Of the many historic sites we visited in Europe, the cathedrals stood out. Some windows had semi-clear panes like Mont-Saint-Michel or the Dom in Germany. The lofty Dom cathedral dominates the vista with two huge spires reaching skyward, and a smaller one nestled between them. Moving closer to the building, the intricate stonework and windows become visible. Every opening is etched in layers of stone that dwarf the windows. The Dom took over 600 years to complete; the men who started it never saw their work finished. Other cathedrals were filled with beautiful stained glass like Notre-Dame of Paris. Each abbey, built by craftsmen trying to capture the majesty of God, inspires respect, worship, and devotion to the Lord Almighty.

Once inside, monasteries are often lofty and dark with little light penetrating their depths. Worshipers and visitors are naturally drawn to the windows as they let in sunlight. No matter how wondrous or stately, cathedrals are only a poor copy of the majesty of God. Jesus calls Himself the Light of the World. A stained-glass pane acts only as a pointer to the authentic Light.

Similarly, the buttery yellow fabric diamonds peek out from the white background of the Cathedral Window quilt. Its shape is like light streaming through diamond window panes. Cathedral windows—whether cut in glass and stone or stitched into cloth—let the light into dark places. Sometimes the light is dim, but it is still there. Only Jesus can shine His light into our dark places and guide us as we learn to walk consistently in His way and truth.

My Prayer

Jesus, I love seeing the light come through the windows. I want my heart to be like a cathedral window that shines inside and out with Your holy light. I want Your truth to penetrate the depths of my being. Let Your ways guide me and help me point others to You.

My Response

Lord, send forth Your light and Your truth and
let them guide me.

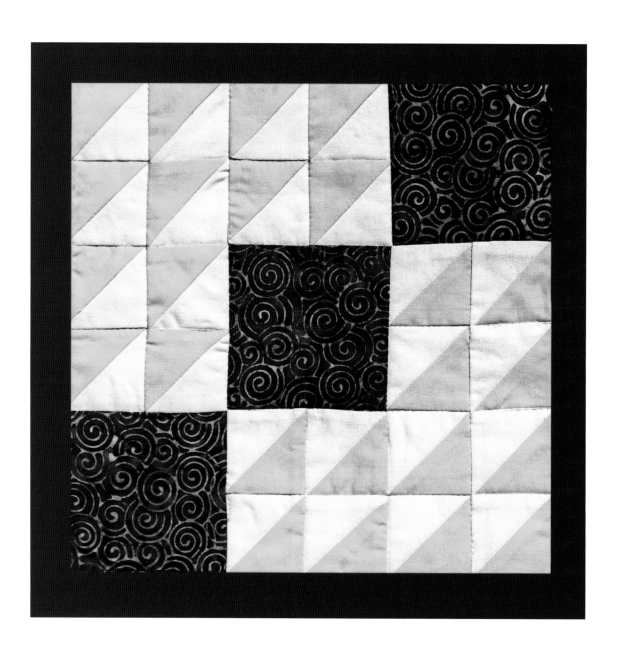

CUT GLASS DISH

Philippians 1:3-6—*I thank my God every time I remember you. In all my prayers for all of you, I always pray with joy because of your partnership in the gospel from the first day until now, being confident of this, that he who began a good work in you will carry it on to completion until the day of Christ Jesus.*

Y ou should write them," my aunt Mary had urged me when I arrived in Dallas. Once I was settled, I wrote to my father's cousins Shirley and Barbara who lived nearby, though we'd never met. I mentioned I was attending the University of North Texas. Within days I was surprised to receive a four-page letter from Shirley, full of warmth and connections. My university choice for my master's happened to be *their* alma mater! During my first break, I arranged to meet the two sisters. They greeted me at the door with hugs and asked if I wanted coffee. I *knew* we were related. We laughed over the family story of how our grandpa Jester, who owned a lunchroom in New Canaan, Connecticut, during the Depression, brought his own coffee grinder and mug with him wherever he went in case a cuppa Joe wasn't available.

As we sat down to a beautifully laid table for lunch, we traded stories easily. We discovered a common deep faith in Christ as well as the family bond. Before I left, both cousins presented me with gifts they'd received from my grandmother. Shirley gave me a candy dish with silver edging. Barbara presented me with a cut glass dish with a ten-petal floral design etched in its base. She enclosed a note: "Your grandmother, my auntie Gertrude, sent this lovely crystal bowl as a wedding present. I have used it these many years as a true favorite. I want you to have it and enjoy." Tears sprang from my eyes. I was overwhelmed to receive such personal gifts from these dear women I'd just met.

Shirley and Barbara's faith, kindness, and Southern hospitality were an encouragement to me. Our first visit, and the many that followed while I was in Texas for two years, showed me how intricate the plan of God is for my life. I had new sisters in the faith—and the love of family—while I lived away from home. I have thanked God often for the joy of knowing them and the unexpected link to my grandmother.

My Dallas cousins are a reminder to me that God is always at work. Their gifts sparkle as I use them in my home. Tiny cuts in the crystal bowl catch the light just as the tiny triangles in the Cut Glass Dish quilt draw the eye inward along the points. As a glass cutter crafts a beautiful piece of art with precision, a skilled quilter creates a wondrous pattern from intricate cuts and stitches. Likewise, God crafts us into His "good works" and artfully sets us in the right place among the right people in the right season.

My Prayer

Lord, my life is so rich. Thank You for the affection of family and friends. I pray for each of them and thank You for their faithfulness. Keep my loved ones strong so that we can all rejoice on that day when You finish Your great work in us.

My Response

He who began a good work in me will carry it on to completion!

DOVE IN THE WINDOW

1 Corinthians 2:10-11—these are the things God has revealed to us by his Spirit. The Spirit searches all things, even the deep things of God. For who knows a person's thoughts except their own spirit within them? In the same way no one knows the thoughts of God except the Spirit of God.

A pair of white ceramic doves and a vase of fresh cut flowers sit on a side table next to the big picture window. The owner of the charming, turn-of-the-century house on State Street is often out in her yard tending to the garden. Over the years, I've watched her watering the roses, weeding or laying down pavers. As I've passed by on my walks, a brown wicker chair looks inviting on her front porch and those little doves catch my eye and make me smile.

Doves are often seen as symbols of love and peace. They are also messengers. In the Bible story about Noah, a dove was released after the Flood to help the passengers on the ark find dry land. The bird came back. "When the dove returned to him in the evening, there in its beak was a freshly plucked olive leaf," records Genesis 8:11. This well-known story may have been the inspiration for the Dove in the Window quilt pattern, which dates back to the 1890s. Four triangle-shaped doves press into a square window in the center of the quilt block.

For the Christian, the dove also symbolizes the Holy Spirit. In the Gospel accounts, the Spirit descended from Heaven in the form of a dove during the baptism of Jesus. After His crucifixion and resurrection, Jesus promised to send His followers a helper. The Holy Spirit is the fulfillment of that promise. He is our comforter and approaches our hearts with the gentleness of a dove. He lightens our burdens and calms our fears. The Holy Spirit reminds us of God's written Word. His constant, loving presence in our lives is like the morning light flooding in a window.

Like a dove waiting on the sill, we can invite the Spirit into our life. As God's holy messenger, the Spirit's voice and healing ways are dovelike: gentle, faithful, loving, bringing peace. The Spirit also searches all things in our hearts. As the gardener carefully tends her roses, the Comforter attends to the growth, needs, and cries of our soul. Through the Spirit, we have new life in Jesus. We can take great comfort knowing that we are fully known and never alone. The same Counselor that knows the thoughts of Almighty God knows us.

My Prayer

Lord, teach me to depend on Your Spirit in my life. Help me invite You into my everyday thoughts and activities. Thank you for Your wisdom and comfort. I want Your precious and holy presence to cleanse, heal, and nurture my soul.

My Response

I know the Spirit searches all things, even the deep things of God.

30

FLOWER BASKET

Romans 12:6-8—*We have different gifts, according to the grace given to each of us. If your gift is prophesying, then prophesy in accordance with your faith; if it is serving, then serve; if it is teaching, then teach; if it is to encourage, then give encouragement; if it is giving, then give generously; if it is to lead, do it diligently; if it is to show mercy, do it cheerfully.*

The doorbell rang. My friend greeted me with a bucket filled with an assortment of roses, freshly cut from his garden. With obvious pride, he explained their various names as I gushed over their beauty. A true rose aficionado, Brian has several dozen bushes, which he carefully tends. As I arranged the flowers in a vase, I felt their smooth petals, cool to the touch. I trimmed the stem of an Ingrid Bergman, a deep red rose with clusters of partially-opened blossoms. My favorite was a Fragrant Lace, a yellow-white rose with magenta-tinted edges. Another called Brandy, with tangerine blossoms, pink edges, and ragged petals, charmed me with its beauty. The lone lavender Harlequin was wilting, but was so lovely. I cut the ends of a bundle of wine-colored rosebuds named Legend. I admired my arrangement. I was in awe of God's creativity, realizing this was just a handful of countless varieties of roses.

Like the myriad flower species God has created, He lavishes upon His children a variety of talents and kinds of beauty. Each of us is unique in our makeup of personality, physical features, ambitions, dreams, life experiences, and family history. The variety—our unique color and fragrance—makes us individually beautiful.

Developing and utilizing our spiritual and natural gifts give our life purpose and joy. As we share our gifts of encouraging, teaching, giving, serving, or leading, we bloom and bless others. Our combination of gifts is a bouquet for others to behold. In God's economy, our abilities and beauty never detract from another's. Like the roses, all of us have distinct qualities to be admired.

Like the Flower Basket quilt, the color and patterns of fabric add interest to the quilt's overall uniform design. Just as each colorful scrap selected to piece the baskets may have a special origin or story behind it, our skills and experiences make us precious to God and to each other. We can find joy knowing our life is carefully crafted—and tended—by a loving Designer.

My Prayer

*Dear God, help me see my special place in Your flower basket.
I want to fully enjoy the way You created me. Please don't let me
envy another's blossoms if they appear to be brighter. Instead let me
appreciate the gifts You've given to others. Let my heart be filled with
the fragrance of Christ. May the color and beauty You add to my life
spill over generously to my friends and family.*

My Response

I have different gifts, according to the grace given me.

34

GARDEN PATH

1 Corinthians 13:4-7—*Love is patient, love is kind. It does not envy, it does not boast, it is not proud. It does not dishonor others, it is not self-seeking, it is not easily angered, it keeps no record of wrongs. Love does not delight in evil but rejoices with the truth. It always protects, always trusts, always hopes, always perseveres.*

I stood looking out the window into my mother's summer garden. The sunlight filtering down through the canopy of trees gave the garden a dappled appearance. Some of the leaves were in full sun, shimmering a translucent green. Others were half in the sun and half in the shade. A coral Tropicana rose was highlighted in full sun, while other roses on the same bush were muted. Daisies played peek-a-boo with the leaves of the Siberian iris, their white heads a sharp contrast to the deep green. The bright pink of the impatiens, tucked in and around the gravel path, glowed in the sunlight.

I sighed, wishing that I could capture all of the glory of the garden year-round. I wondered if other women felt the same way and if that inspired the design of the Garden Path quilt. Perhaps anticipating the dark winter months, women captured the light, beauty, and color of the flowers to be enjoyed when the plants lie dormant.

Each of the individual flowers my mother selected makes her whole garden more beautiful. However, a thoughtfully planted garden takes feeding, weeding, and pruning. Like a careful gardener, Jesus plants and nurtures His love in our hearts and brings a variety of people into our lives. Some are like the sunshine and rich soil and cause us to thrive and grow. A friend's timely encouragement and compassion can be water to our souls.

Jesus also watches for the weeds or pests that ruin the garden. Negative character traits like resentment, conceit, or cross words can start as seedlings in our hearts. Jesus constantly works at weeding out envy, pride, and anger from our character. If these traits are left unchecked to grow in the soil of our hearts, they will choke out the beauty and the fragrance of the flowers of love. The cherished plants will grow sickly and die. Any plant must be cut back to force more blooms. Sometimes Jesus uses challenging people or circumstances to stimulate the growth of love. As we generously respond and react to others, He strengthens and enlarges our hearts.

Does our heart's garden reflect the compassion of Jesus? Each seedling has the opportunity to grow into patience, kindness, gentleness, and self-control. Are we open to letting Him work in our hearts to plant His love and weed out the things that keep it from growing? Like the Garden Path quilt, which captures the beautiful blooms of summer in patches and threads, our hearts can hold and display the beauty and fragrance of Christ.

My Prayer

Jesus, as I look at a well-kept garden, I am reminded that it didn't happen on its own. Lots of care went into choosing the plants and deciding where they would be planted. I want You to plant Your love in my life. Help me to respond to others with Your kindness. I give You permission to weed out my negative attitudes so that Your character will be seen in me.

My Response

Love always protects, always trusts, always hopes,
always perseveres...

GARDEN WALK

Matthew 26:39—*Going a little farther, he fell with his face to the ground and prayed, "My Father, if it is possible, may this cup be taken from me. Yet not as I will, but as you will."*

I *hate this, I hate it, I hate it!* I sobbed as I huddled under the Garden Walk quilt, tears streaming down my face. It was 2:30 AM. My family was asleep. I sat alone in the dark with pain rippling down my leg from my hip to my foot. I was enduring another night of misery. I despise what persistent pain does and the limitations it forces upon my life. Coping with this unrelenting companion causes a constant drain on my energy. I struggle with the cost it imposes on my family, like missing trips or not participating in activities with them. There are times I detest what I see in myself, the quick way I snap at others because I hurt or how I settle into a spiral of negative thoughts. Hugging the quilt tighter, I waited for the medication to take effect. Resting my head on my arms, the green, white, and yellow points of the quilt blurred together through my tears.

The Garden Walk quilt reminds me of another long-ago struggle with suffering. Jesus wrestled with the Father about accepting that cup of sorrow in the Garden of Gethsemane. Christ endured the overwhelming agony and distress being poured out on Him. He faced a painful death on the cross. He didn't want to hurt any more than I want to hurt, but He could see the outcome of it all. Jesus saw past the pain to us—and the salvation He would purchase for each of us with His blood.

So, like Jesus, I'm in the garden of choice. I don't like this companion called pain. Although I don't have the option of rejecting it, I can control how it affects my life and those around me. I can choose to see how Jesus embraces me as I am and learn to accept my situation. Standing at the crossroads, I can focus on my affliction or focus on the One Who has endured. He sees the essence of who I am in this condition and loves me. He reaches out to me with unlimited comfort, understanding, and strength.

Just as Jesus saw past the agony of His own suffering, He can help us see past it in our lives. He might not take it away, but through His strength we can express thankfulness for the relationship we have with Him. We can look for ways in which He will use our distress as the means to know Him better. He can change our focus from the pain to the One Who overcomes.

My Prayer

Dear Jesus, I desire with all my heart to dash this cup of suffering away from me. I don't like hurting. Yet I think of Your decision as You wrestled with pain. You chose to accept what Your Father was asking. Help me to be like You and accept the difficult seasons in my life.

My Response

Not my will, but as You will, Jesus…

GRANDMOTHER'S FAN

Isaiah 33:6—*He will be the sure foundation for your times, a rich store of salvation and wisdom and knowledge; the fear of the LORD is the key to this treasure.*

L aughter drifted on the breeze as the ladies paddled the water highway of the Snoqualmie. Their canoes slipped along the river as the autumn sunlight flickered through the golden red leaves of the trees to the water below. Beaching their canoes, they hiked up the trail to the log cabin tucked amongst the tall cedars.

As the women gathered inside the cabin, they stretched the quilt out on the frame and prepared to complete Grandmother's Fan. The partial circles lay across the corner of each square, resembling an open handheld fan. The shades of greens and pinks of the fan were a soft contrast to the white background. It was 1890 and they were finishing a quilt that would be raffled off to provide funds to build their new church.

Throughout its history, women have helped the church in the Snoqualmie Valley traverse the river of time. As decades passed, women faced struggles such as isolation in a new territory, wars, financial difficulty, or the drastic change from a rural to a suburban community. While circumstances may change, each generation of women sought to impart the unchanging values and wisdom of God to the next.

Although our grandmothers faced different situations, we all have struggles and hopes in common. We all long for friendship, the ability to dream, and to grow in our faith in Christ. God is the same for each generation. Just as the layers of fabric make a single covering, each woman adds her own unique block and stitches to the overall creation. In Grandmother's Fan, the colors reflect the repeated design; however, the quilting displays the crafter's personal style. Her stitches might be long or short, or not quite uniform across the entire block, but each stitch holds the material together.

Just as women pass on the legacy of quilting, so we hand down the legacy of our faith. Jesus Christ is a rich store of salvation, great wisdom, and a sure foundation for all of our times. Like our grandmothers, we have a chance to add our block to the quilt of eternity. As each block is placed in the quilt, the pattern is consistent with the unbroken design. When our descendants look back over our life, hopefully they will see how our heart was intertwined and anchored to the Master quilter.

My Prayer

Lord, I want to be a woman who faithfully creates a beautiful block to be added to the quilt of time. I long to help others find and discover the design You have given to us. Thank you that You are faithful to each generation and that I get to be part of Your beautiful workmanship that lasts for all time.

My Response

My fear of the Lord is the key to wisdom and knowledge.

46

HANDS ALL AROUND

Ecclesiastes 4:9-10—*Two are better than one, because they have a good return for their labor: If either of them falls down, one can help the other up. But pity anyone who falls and has no one to help them up.*

My mother held up her arms to receive her young grandson, James. Settling into the rocker, she gave him her pointer finger and he wrapped his small fist around it. Smiling, I watched them contentedly rock back and forth. On the wall behind them hung the sample quilt of Hands All Around. Shades of blue and white fabric pieces reflected four hands reaching out from a center square. At the tip of each palm were fingers made from the points of triangles.

Gazing at my own hands, I pondered all the things I do with them. Among other things, they are used for helping, healing, playing, reaching, and protecting. I regarded the tableau my mom and son made. As we age, we use our hands in different ways. Although a baby grasps, a child learns to reach out to hold a hand for protection. A teen still needs the hand of guidance. As adults we learn to give back as well as take, thus completing the cycle.

The quilt block shows hands that reach outwards, like a circle of friends seeking comfort, direction, and encouragement from each other. I think of all the women in my life that have strengthened my heart and helped guide me along difficult paths. Their hands have held mine in prayer during times of decision, sorrow, and joy. They have provided meals or a touch of encouragement when it was so desperately needed.

One gives, one receives, and the cycle goes on and on. Sometimes we are a giver and sometimes a receiver, yet we are always reaching towards one another. In the Hands All Around quilt, the open palms are giving and receiving and are connected by a band of color around a square. Perhaps that center square represents the heart of our life, Jesus Christ.

There are indeed hands all around us. One longs to reach out, others long to help, some seek to encourage, and still other hands just need someone else's to hold on to. We can allow our lives to be the hands of Jesus as we hold out His life to others. As we move through the seasons of our own life, He is our strong foundation and source of strength. Through Him, we have the ability to give to others as well as learn to receive from Him. Jesus is the center that connects us all together.

My Prayer

*Jesus, I think about all of the hands that have touched mine. Some
I remember clearly, others are lost to time, yet each one has impacted
my life. You have used so many lives to shape me into the person
I am today. I want to be someone who has the ability to both give and
receive. I want an open heart that reaches toward You
and to those around me.*

My Response

Two are better than one...if my friend falls down,
I can help them up!

HOME TREASURE

Matthew 6:21—*For where your treasure is, there your heart will be also.*

I love opening my door, watching the room fill with guests, and entertaining. I enjoy serving meals on the green, rose, and cream-colored pieces of my Desert Rose dinnerware. It's fun to mix and match napkins and tablecloths with the classic Franciscan design. Another relaxing pastime is decorating my home. I fill it with treasured art and souvenirs—anything that captures memories from an outing or the spirit of a special trip. In decorating, I like adding colors and textures and pairing antiques with classic pieces of furniture. My hallway is lined with framed family photos. One evening my sister Laura and nephew Jordan were over. "I feel really comfortable at your place. I like it here," Jordan said. He made my day.

Décor can create a warm, inviting atmosphere. Likewise, the quilter also carefully selects fabrics and geometric designs to create a unique masterpiece. Some scraps are laden with memories while others are chosen for their patterns or colors. Home Treasure, a classic quilt pattern from the 1890s, uses a combination of triangles and squares to frame a diamond. Within the diamond's borders is a smaller square that looks like a door. Like a hostess who opens her house to guests, the small square door opens the diamond. As a home is filled with beloved possessions, the quilt's center could symbolize the treasures of the heart.

My home is a collection of my treasures. I love to entertain, but my most important guest is Jesus Christ. As a sacred member in my home and heart—does He *feel* welcome and comfortable? What does it take to be a great hostess, or better yet, a good friend? It takes time, attention to your visitor's needs, and a spirit of openness and hospitality to create a comfortable environment. When you invite family or friends over, you naturally spend time with them. You talk with them. You anticipate and meet their needs. Jesus, as our holy guest, is much the same. We need to be open with a desire to talk to Him each day. What does Christ want and need? He simply asks for our undivided heart, our time, and our love.

As we accept Jesus as the chief resident in our lives, He begins adorning our soul. He adds character qualities like beauty, gentleness, peace, and hope. When Jesus is comfortably at home in our hearts, His love spills over into everything we do. As we get to know Him over time, He buries His ways and His words deep within the fabric of our souls. Like the quilter layers fabrics to create her masterpiece, Jesus lovingly layers into our memories a deep gratitude for His work.

My Prayer

Lord, I want to care for the priceless riches of my heart like I care for the precious things in my home. I spend so much time dusting and rearranging my belongings. I want to treat You like the diamond that You are and make You feel welcome in the home of my heart. Help me open its door wide for You.

My Response

For where my treasure is, my heart will be also!

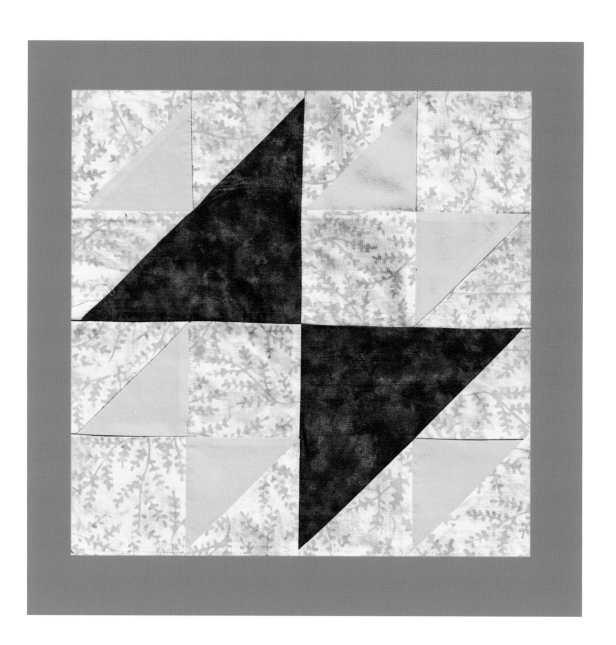

HOURGLASS

Psalm 90:12—*Teach us to number our days, that we may gain a heart of wisdom.*

Shrieking kids jumped around in delight as the dark sky above them exploded in shimmering colors. Trails of light sparkled downward as loud booms reverberated in the air. Dancing with exuberance, the neighborhood children thoroughly enjoyed the fireworks show. Earlier that day I watched my son focus laser-like on the leaves of a tree as he scrutinized their veins, color, and texture. The young have an innate ability to live for the moment. They can easily stop and examine a bug on the path, follow a snail's trail or imagine themselves as part of the fireworks. They don't worry about the time of day, what they will do tomorrow or even what they will eat. Instead, they trust the adults in their world for the food, clothes, and routine that they need.

Straightening up the house after the Fourth of July party, I flipped the Hourglass quilt open onto the bed. My eyes traced the green squares, gold and purple triangles, and the detailed stitching around the design. Smoothing it out, I glanced again at the hourglass figures flung across the quilt. They are a reminder of the slipping sands of time and that our journey is short. Just as the quilter determines a set quantity of blocks before she declares it complete, so we have only a finite number of years before our work will cease.

Unlike a child, I can easily get caught up in yesterday and tomorrow, never quite having enough time for the present. Perhaps that is why the Creator wants us to live in the moment. He desires that we delight in the things that He has placed in our lives: the monarchs flitting by in the garden, the early morning sun creating shadow plays on the wall, or joining in the spontaneous laughter of children. Instead, I dwell on what happened yesterday and try to second-guess how it will impact today—or I pitch myself forward into tomorrow as I live in the what-ifs.

The Bible says to number our days, to look around and realize that we only have this small slice of time in which to fully live. When we concentrate on the past or worry for the future, we rob ourselves of today. Yesterday or tomorrow are like fine drops of mist that dissolve in our hands as we try to grasp them. We need a heart of wisdom to remember that only this moment is ours; we can stop and enjoy it or reach for the mist as it melts away.

My Prayer

Jesus, help me to have a wise heart to understand that I only have today. Help me to remember that just like a quilter might take months or years to complete her project, eventually it will be finished. In the same way, one day my life will be complete. Help me to stop spending my time on regrets and what-ifs, but to rejoice and seek You in every moment.

My Response

Teach me to number my days so that I may
have a discerning heart.

KALEIDOSCOPE

Isaiah 26:3—*You will keep in perfect peace those whose minds are steadfast, because they trust in you.*

The whirl of colors, lights, and sounds came from carnival vendors hawking their wares and games at the state fairgrounds. Their loud and insistent tones created a blur of noise and it was difficult to track with any one of them at a time. Just as I was able to focus in on one, another blared disruptively, demanding attention and adding to the confusion. I soon slipped from the din of the amusement aisles to the quiet hush of the quilters' exhibition hall.

Admiring the hanging quilts on display, one work of art caught my eye. Vibrant colors danced across the Kaleidoscope quilt top. The materials alternated from dark to light, with each square creating a shifting and colorful pattern. Sometimes the dark colors came forward, accentuating the points of the fabric, yet other times the light ones stood out. The design seemed to vibrate as the diamonds in the middle of the square suddenly came into focus. The Kaleidoscope quilt was an exciting and elusive design.

Like the chaos of a carnival or the swirling colors of a kaleidoscope, the "urgent" screams for our time. The constant tug of family, home, and work can contribute to a lack of balance. Each claim seems to yell louder than the first until it is hard to know which way to turn. Our hearts cry out for direction, stability, and rest. Yet round and round we go, without a central focal point from which to orchestrate the confusion. We are spun by a merry-go-round of movement and demands. How do we make it stop?

Jesus Christ offers stability and brings the spinning colors of our kaleidoscope into sharp focus. Like the light colors of the quilt squares, Jesus adds His perspective and balance to the dark corners of our hearts. Only when we stop and look intently at Jesus can the confusing whirl be transformed into His design. He can help us push the dark colors back into their defined places by adding His light hues of rest, peace, and hope. Through His Word, love, and unchanging ways, Jesus desires to help us find balance for our lives.

My Prayer

Lord Jesus, my life often whirls out of focus. The colors run together and blur and I need Your help in defining the perspective of my life. I want to concentrate on things that are valuable and lasting, not just those that clamor for my time and energy in the here and now. I need to have Your eternal perspective. I want to live my life for You.

My Response

I will stay in perfect peace as I trust in You.

LONE STAR

Philippians 2:14-16—*Do everything without grumbling or arguing, so that you may become blameless and pure, "children of God without fault in a warped and crooked generation." Then you will shine among them like stars in the sky as you hold firmly to the word of life. And then I will be able to boast on the day of Christ that I did not run or labor in vain.*

I slowly traced the eight-pointed Lone Star pattern with my finger. Warmly, I thought about my grandmother's loving hands that had worked over the quilt, hands now stilled and quieted for eternity. The dark-colored star stood out vividly from its white background. *How does the Lone Star reflect my grandmother's life?* I thought. *In what ways did she stand out from other women around her?*

At age 55, Grandma Fern had put her faith in Christ. On that day, she became a child of God. As she grew in her relationship with Christ, she became less afraid to tell others about Him. Sometimes, due to sleeplessness, she'd get up and walk the floors and pray. Things would change when I asked Grandma to pray.

My grandmother's life shone like a star. Despite her failing health, I never heard her complain or argue. She displayed a gentle, courageous spirit, yet laughed easily, and was fun to be with. In spite of her pain, she did not call attention to herself, but put others at ease.

I rose to retrieve Grandma's letters stored in a dusty box. Reading several, I smiled as they retold her adventures of cross-country skiing in Colorado (way into her seventies!), spending time in the garden, staying busy with neighbors and Bible studies, and keeping in touch with family. Her words of warmth and encouragement came alive again through the pages of her letters. Putting them down and smoothing out the surface of the quilt, I realized that Grandma's life was like the Lone Star because she emanated the eternal beauty of Jesus Christ.

God has scattered millions of stars across the heavens, and some shine brighter than others. Like the Lone Star stitched on a contrasting background, Jesus shines a bright light in a dark and broken world. He stands apart and reflects the true light and love of God. Like the bright stars that directed travelers in ages past, Jesus guides today's weary travelers to His Father.

My Prayer

Lord, I want to be like the Lone Star that stands out against its background. Let me shine brightly like the stars in the universe as I walk along the paths You have designed. I need the courage to stand apart for You! Jesus, may I display Your light and beauty to those around me.

My Response

I do everything without complaining or arguing…
I am a child of God!

LOVE KNOT

John 15:12-13—*My command is this: Love each other as I have loved you. Greater love has no one than this: to lay down one's life for one's friends.*

The quilt was spread over the mahogany four-poster in the guest bedroom. Its colors were striking shades of green, tan, ivory, and light pink. I asked my friend to tell me about the design of rectangles and squares. "It's called 'Love Knot,'" she replied. "Is there a story behind this quilt?" I asked.

"My mom, my sisters, and aunts worked together for over a year to make me this quilt," she said. "They kept it a secret and gave it to me on my fiftieth birthday!" Each person working on the quilt had a special tie to her—ties secured in love.

Knots of love are formed at different times in our lives and in different ways with different people. Some are linked together early in childhood with family and friends.

Still others come as we grow in our lives and relationships or as we unite with a spouse and have our own families. Each bond leaves something of ourselves with another, just as two parts of a string are entwined together. Some cords are tied tightly and never to be loosened, yet others seem to slip apart easily.

As I think about the love knots in my life, images of people important to me come to mind: my grandparents, parents, siblings, my spouse, my child, and cherished friends. Some are now gone. All of these ties have made an impression upon my life. They are helping me to become the person that I am by weaving a background of acceptance, support, and love.

Among these relationships, the most important love knot in my life is one that was tied as a young girl. That love knot was tied with Jesus Christ. He offered me His part of the knot when He died for my sins. I took His part and offered myself to Him by accepting His death, resurrection, and love. By that simple, yet profound act, my life is bound to His forever.

Jesus, as the Master in tying love knots, longs to have that bond with us. Once that knot is secured with Him, He begins to teach us how to create successful bonds with our families and friends. He shows us how to love each other unconditionally. He gives us opportunities in a variety of relationships to express kindness, faithfulness, gentleness, and patience. Christ, the author of love, is the eternal bond in the love knots of our lives.

My Prayer

Lord Jesus, teach me to love others just as You have loved me. Your love holds me securely and will never let me slip away. Sometimes my love knots are so frail; sometimes they even fail. I can rest my whole life in You and know that You will never give way. Please teach me how to love. Thank You for being the most beautiful love knot of all.

My Response

Teach me to love as Jesus has loved me!

MEMORY BLOCK

Proverbs 22:6—*Start children off on the way they should go, and even when they are old they will not turn from it.*

We had just moved to Washington State when I entered the first grade. My practical, gentle mother pinned a scrap of paper to my jacket, which read, "My name is Ellen. If I am lost, I ride bus number 87." This was in case I forgot how to get home in all the excitement and chaos of my first few days in a new school. I chafed at the idea of the note being safety-pinned to my chest. Did my mother think I was a baby or something? The simple message had that return-to-sender brevity to it.

However, it did the trick. One day amidst the noise and shuffle of children blasting out of classrooms toward the row of waiting buses, I didn't know which yellow bus to board. Soon a kindly teacher was guiding me by the elbow toward Bus 87. Happy to see the familiar face of my driver, I never forgot that number ever again. As an older child, I used to see Bus 87 roll down the neighborhood streets. I often recalled my sense of relief of having been returned to my right path. *I ride bus number 87.* I marvel now at my mother's wise insistence, overriding my childish plea to be "grown up" and not have to wear such a silly note.

Just as my mother's simple and gentle ways are etched in my heart, the affection and goodwill of family and friends are stitched into the Memory Block quilt. It is a popular pattern to give as a gift to a loved one moving away. Rows of tiny triangles form a frame for embroidering or stenciling a message. A simple "I love you" or "Your friend always" will be viewed often once travelers depart.

As the Memory Block quilt pattern bears the signatures and love of friends, God's ways and decrees are written on my heart. *Jesus loves me this I know, for the Bible tells me so* is a comforting refrain from childhood that also plays in my mind. Accepting His sacrificial love for me returned me to the right path. His love is more than safety-pinned to my chest; it's embedded deep in my soul. I once was lost; now I am found. His Holy Spirit guides and prompts our spirits to seek His truth. Jesus may use people, Scripture, songs, or experiences to draw us to the Father. Our souls know deep relief when we find Him. His message is simple: *Follow me.* Gladly, once we do, we will not turn from Him.

My Prayer

God, thank you for the blessing of memory and the comfort I find in recalling Your provisions. You have trained me up and watched over me since I was a child. I may not have been aware of Your love, but now I keep You close at hand and heart. Draw me near to You and may I never leave Your side.

My Response

Train me, God, in the way I should go.

MILKY WAY

Isaiah 40:26—*Lift your eyes and look to the heavens: Who created all these? He who brings out the starry host one by one and calls them each by name. Because of his great power and mighty strength, not one of them is missing.*

A scent of smoke, toasted marshmallows, and hot chocolate wafted on the evening breeze as I stepped away from the campfire. The hushed voices of my family mingled with the snap and crackle of the fire. Their dark forms silhouetted against its bright flames. Camping far from city lights, the Arizona night sky shared its majestic secrets. Gazing upwards, I took in the splendor of the gossamer appearance of the Milky Way, wishing that I could somehow hold onto what I was observing. Scores of stars were scattered across the velvety black of space like celestial jewels.

Visible or not, the starry host faithfully appears in the sky each evening. Perhaps capturing the heavenly beauties was what compelled quilters long ago to recreate the Milky Way in fabric. The exact placement of the blue and gold triangles and squares imparts an illusion of stars scattered across the quilt's surface. Just as the shapes are precisely placed on the quilt, the nighttime vista is also stretched out against the dark sky with the skill of an artist.

Anyone would notice if one tiny piece of a quilt is missing. Yet among the millions of stars, would we notice if one was absent? The Milky Way is filled with countless stars and is just one of thousands of galaxies that exist in space. As incredible as it seems, God calls each by name. As He brings them out at nightfall, not one is missing from the procession. In His great power, He calls, holds, and places each star in its own spot. His pattern for space is not random but crafted with great precision.

Like the stars, we are individually known to the Creator God. He calls each of us by name and longs for us to respond to Him. Like the stars, He knows if we are missing from His presence. Will we choose to answer His gentle call? Perhaps the women who designed the Milky Way quilt sought to capture the majesty of God. Using our own lives as the fabric, His power, strength, and beauty can be displayed and reflected to those around us.

My Prayer

Jesus, You are the artist who carefully places the stars in their locations as the sun sets. I marvel that You know each of them by name. I am amazed that you know me by name and call me to shine for You. May I wholeheartedly respond to You. May my life declare the beauty of Who You are and be seen by others.

My Response

I lift my eyes and look to the heavens…I know my Creator!

MOSAIC

Genesis 16:13—*[Hagar] gave this name to the LORD who spoke to her: "You are the God who sees me," for she said, "I have now seen the One who sees me."*

Rushing to get the room ready for my longtime friend, I knocked a box of photos off the desk and the images scattered all over the floor. As I started to pick them up I was pulled into looking at them. The snapshots captured different aspects of my life: wife, mother, daughter, sister, aunt, and friend. Smiling, I placed them back in the box and reached for the maroon, purple, and pink Mosaic quilt to spread over the guestroom bed.

Just as those photos represent different fragments of my life, the quilt was created from different pieces of fabric cut into squares and triangles. Each snippet of cloth has both a shape and shade of color that can be used to match or contrast with the others. However, without following instructions, the quilter wouldn't know how they fit together to create the finished design.

In the same way, we all have facets of our lives that are defined by our personal interactions. The roles of wife, mother or friend might take center stage for a time. Some demand our attention like the loud, brassy colors of a quilt, while others wait quietly in the background to be noticed. I rush around cramming all my responsibilities into my life, spending time here, but ending up neglecting another area. The colors and shapes of my roles began to blur as I try to hold them all together. I wonder: Who am I? How do I even know what part to play?

Looking at all the pieces, I try to figure out where I belong. Like a quilter, I pick them up and turn them over in my hands seeking to find out where to add this, how the colors will match, and what my life is going to become. I realize I won't know until I follow the pattern. I need to turn to Jesus. He understands all the demands for my time, and as Master Designer, He sees me not as a role but in my entirety. The Creator says that not only does He hold our pieces, but He longs to *be* our everlasting peace.

Taking one last look at the room, I enjoy the Mosaic quilt on the bed. Although the pattern is busy, each piece adds to the entire creation. One square or one triangle is not more noticeable than its neighbor. Likewise, following Him, all the pieces of who we are will also fit into His divine plan for us. God gives us the strength and ability to be a spouse, parent, sibling, child or friend. He also helps us maintain His perspective and balance in our lives.

My Prayer

Jesus, the roles in my life clamor to be noticed. I often forget that I am more than what I do. I belong to You, and You can help me when all my responsibilities are loudly demanding pieces of my life. Help me to keep them in balance and to know when and where to give. Help me to remember that I am Yours and that You are the One Who sees me.

My Response

I have now seen the One Who sees me…

OCEAN WAVE

Joshua 23:8—*But you are to hold fast to the Lord your God, as you have until now.*

My cat jumped for the window sill and missed. He and the quilt rack came crashing to the floor. With his fur puffed out and tail straight up, Zippy shot out of the room while I picked up the rack and straightened the quilts. As I reached for one of my favorite comforters, Ocean Wave, I thought about the times that I have spent by the sea.

Memories of those vacations swirled in my thoughts like the waves breaking around the rocky outcroppings. I thought about times of walking along the Oregon beach and building sandcastles. I remembered dashing in and out among the waves and exploring tidal pools with my family. I recalled the feeling of peace flooding my soul as we watched a silvery moon set across the Pacific.

As the tide goes out, marine life that is usually unseen becomes approachable in easy-to-reach pools. The creatures are dependent on the changing tide as the churning, swirling waters pounding the pools cause them to be left standing almost dry or completely under water. The sea provides life-giving waves filled with food. The animals that live within this harsh environment have adapted to the changing flow of the ocean.

Like the ebb and flow of the ocean tide, the shattering breakers of change swirl around my life. I might find myself in a stale pool of boredom and monotony or in water over my head with stress and responsibility. I may feel the tugging waves of discouragement and hopelessness and desire to yield to its pull. I remind myself of the starfish and anemones fiercely clinging to the rocks.

Just as the blue-and-white fabric triangles seem to swirl around the Ocean Wave quilt, the breakers in our lives can push us to hold on to Jesus, our steadfast Rock. Like the sea creatures, we need to accept the pools and know that the stale or deep waters will change. Unlike the marine life, in the fierce pull of the waves we can choose to give up. In times of despair, it is tempting to let go and drift away from all we know. However, we can choose to hold fast to Jesus with all our might knowing that He is stronger and able to steady us through the changing tides of life.

My Prayer

Jesus, some days are just so hard and I long to give up. Is it worth it to keep holding on? Help me to see that these waves are not destroying me, but pushing me towards You. You are my Rock, and only in You do I have the strength to resist the fierce tugging. You never change; this is my comfort.

My Response

I will hold fast to the Lord my God.

86

OHIO STAR

Romans 15:5-6—*May the God who gives endurance and encouragement give you the same attitude of mind toward each other that Christ Jesus had, so that with one mind and one voice you may glorify the God and Father of our Lord Jesus Christ.*

As I slit the envelope, tiny swatches of fabric fluttered to the table. Turning the envelope over, I smiled as the Canadian stamp and postmark caught my eye. Joni shared her excitement for the Ohio Star quilt sampler in sketches and notes: "There's enough colour in each to match the other coloured stars even though individually they are predominantly one colour scheme."

My college friend presented me with the finished quilt last Christmas. The gift, a year in the making, is precious on many levels. Embedded in this quilt is more than 30 years of friendship and our shared successes and heartaches. The block pattern has deep meaning for me as well, since I was born in Ohio and my maternal relatives settled Ohio Territory over 200 years ago.

The Ohio Star's eight triangle points radiate outwards and frame a small square within a larger square. Quilters of days gone by named blocks for people, places, and objects dear to them, for biblical themes or for their home state. Like Joni, quilters select fabrics with complementary and contrasting color schemes. Even swatches that don't seem to match can be worked into a quilt by an artist with a keen eye for balance, unity, and contrast.

Like a quilt's distinct colors, individuals with different talents, beliefs, and backgrounds fill our homes, workplaces, and churches. These contrasts add color and interest to our relationships. Yet how often do we focus only on the differences? Do we treat those who are not just like us as if they were an odd swatch that somehow doesn't match? At times, we might be uncomfortable with their uniqueness. However, it is the blending and contrasting of the elements that create fusion and beauty. The color differences are used to achieve visual balance.

Jesus urges us to experience that elusive spirit of harmony and unity. We can ask God to give us understanding with a family member who is different from us. We can encourage a friend and help her feel comfortable in a new situation. Though we may feel tarnished and unworthy in others' eyes, we can rejoice that Christ loves us and sees our beauty and worth. He chose us from the scrap heap and gave us a new name. In the Creator's skilled hands, a seemingly out-of-place patch is lovingly anchored. Like the triangles on the Ohio Star quilt that touch one another, we all have points of connection to match other "stars" in God's family. In the quilt of His making, we are the colorful swatches that blend together.

My Prayer

Dear God, help me to focus on You and others instead of myself.
In times of stress I seem to see the worst in others and fixate on how
we are not alike. Help me regain Your eternal perspective. May I seek
Your spirit of unity and see how everyone has a part in
Your master quilt.

My Response

God gives me the spirit of unity so that with one heart
and mouth I may glorify Him!

90

PROVIDENCE

Psalm 8:1—*LORD, our Lord, how majestic is your name in all the earth! You have set your glory in the heavens.*

Walking along the lake road in the early morning, I stopped to rest on a damp wooden bench at Kirkland's Houghton Beach. I've come to this park many times over the years. The glimpses of Lake Washington—no matter how often I see it—always fill me. I never tire of sitting near its calming waters, watching small brown birds dart in and out of the shrubs or seagulls pitch and dive overhead or looking at the white birches at shore's edge. Every day there's something new to see. Today, I came across a child's chalk drawing on the sidewalk of a train with smoke billowing, a single boxcar, and caboose. The sky-blue chalk outline is fading under all the foot traffic.

While on my bench, I watched two mallard ducks swim across the calm lake as they appeared out of the grasses. I chuckled to myself as they paddled about fifteen feet and disappeared behind a theater curtain of reeds. When they came out of hiding, this time four mallards appeared. Those four soon swam in the opposite direction and disappeared again behind the marshy drapes. When they reappeared moments later, there were six ducks in procession. Two, four, then six, like a small stage filling up with dancers. Our God has a sense of humor.

The Psalmist David proclaims the majesty of God and that His glory is visible in the heavens. We can look at a lake or to the sky above and see the glory of nature, reminding us that Providence controls both heaven and earth. These bits of beauty and joy on a morning walk remind me of the layers of a quilt. Each fabric scrap is carefully selected by an unseen hand and stands as testament to the efforts of its creator. Likewise, the quilter's expert stitches hold it all together.

The Providence quilt block is formed with a large X and a cross that contains a smaller box in its center. The X points in four directions, with four triangle-tipped arrows pointing toward the heavens. The cross extends outwards and upwards, too. Likewise, whatever direction we look—north, south, east or west—God's glory and majesty are present all around us. He is the unseen power that holds our entire world together. Yet He reaches into our lives daily as He provides the loving touch of a friend, a family member's generous gift of time or the unmistakable beauties of nature. He can show up in a child's simple drawing, reminding us of the innocence and vitality of youth. He presents us with moments of joy that are so personal and meaningful. Each of these gifts guides us back to the protective care of God.

My Prayer

Lord, let me have eyes to see Your provisions in each day. Let me rest in knowing You control events on earth as well as in heaven. My fears and concerns, no matter how big or small, are always under Your loving care. Help me take joy in the many ways You reveal Yourself to me.

My Response

Lord, how majestic is Your name in all the earth!

94

RIGHT HAND OF FRIENDSHIP

1 John 3:17-18—*If anyone has material possessions and sees a brother or sister in need but has no pity on them, how can the love of God be in that person? Dear children, let us not love with words or speech but with actions and in truth.*

The alarm went off at 4:30 AM. I groaned when I saw the time. Then I remembered it was Christmas Day. Stumbling out of bed, I threw on warm clothes, thinking only of more sleep or a Starbucks latte.

En route to the Union Gospel Mission, my friends and I drove around Seattle's Pioneer Square in the dark and dense fog searching for the building. Once inside, we were assigned tasks by the mission staff. The mood picked up as more bleary-eyed volunteers from other churches filed in. At 6 AM the homeless men and a handful of women began lining up for their coffee and a hot breakfast of eggs, bacon, and pancakes.

As each guest passed through to receive their full tray, we tried to catch their eye and greet them with a cheery, "Hello! Merry Christmas!"

Soon my tiredness left me. I felt privileged to be serving these people, hopefully making their day a bit happier. The line moved steadily for nearly two hours. I found myself thinking about each person I met: *Does he have a family? What will she do on Christmas Day? Why is that man's countenance so sad and empty?* Each had their own unique story that led them to the mission. After the guests departed and the dishes were washed, the staff thanked us for our helping hand.

Providing for others in need, without regard for oneself, binds us together. This message of charity is the theme behind the Right Hand of Friendship quilt. The simple block, a dozen triangles forming a square with eight points, could be four sets of hands reaching outwards. Throughout the Gospels, Jesus encourages us to attend to the needs of others. He reminds us that whatever we do for our brothers or sisters, we do for Him. Whether we care for an elderly neighbor or parent, volunteer our time for others, or travel overseas on a humanitarian mission—all of these are ways we extend ourselves and show His love reaching outwards.

Sometimes we may be unwilling to move out of our comfort to serve others. However, the joy of serving—of becoming uncomfortable—is unequaled. Jesus asks us to value each person as if he or she was Christ Himself. As we risk our safety, resources, and ease for one another, Christ honors that sacrifice and counts it as loving service unto Him.

My Prayer

Lord, help me see the people that come into my life as needing Your touch. Show me how to extend Your friendship in ways that will encourage them. Only You know the long and painful road they've taken. When I'm resistant to serve, remind me of all You've given to me. Help me remember that by serving others I am loving You.

My Response

Whatever I do for my brothers and sisters,
I do for Christ.

SHADOW BOX

2 Corinthians 4:7—*But we have this treasure in jars of clay to show that this all-surpassing power is from God and not from us.*

As my friends and I were snooping through a row of antique stores, we came across a dusty, scuffed-up shadow box. It was just what I'd been looking for, and I was excited by my find. It wasn't an antique, but still I bought it. After weeks of cleaning, stripping, and sanding, I chose a soft maple finish for the stain so it would fit into the décor of my study.

Finally, the box was ready to be hung. Gathering my treasures, I tried various pieces of china and my grandmother's ceramic figurines. I chose colored glass vases, a silver dish, and mementos from family travels. I stood back to admire my handiwork. The miniature boxes showed off the pieces well.

Like curios on display, the Shadow Box quilt is a collection of boxes stitched into one quilt square. The contrasting fabrics create the effect of each box containing yet a smaller one. A light fabric center completes each miniature square. Just as a shadow box has limited space for display, our lives have a finite number of years. Daily we must make choices about what is most valuable and worthy of our time.

Like the dealer who salvages old pieces and restores them to their original beauty and value, God lovingly restores people who come to Him a bit dusty, scuffed up, and hurt from life. Often a quilter chooses a set-aside scrap from the ragbag and finds that perfect place for it in her quilt. Likewise, God selects the seemingly useless scraps from our experiences to masterfully design a life of beauty and purpose.

What will we choose to put in our lives? Are we carefully investing in things of lasting value, or do we hastily and fearfully grab at whatever comes our way? Do we realize that how we fill our time—*our* precious shadow box—is making a choice about what is valuable to us?

Jesus Christ wants so much to be on display in our hearts. Are we known for His virtues of joy, forgiveness, and a sense of purpose? Or have we filled our souls with the clutter of hopelessness, bitterness, and a lack of focus? With our permission, Christ cleanses and refines us so that He can display His splendor in us.

My Prayer

Jesus, I want Your presence to be evident in me. Please open up my heart to You. I give You permission to clean and refurbish the shadow box of my heart so that Your loving-kindness and power will shine brilliantly through me.

My Response

This all-surpassing power is from God and not from me.

102

STAR LANE

Psalm 25:15—*My eyes are ever on the Lord, for only he will release my feet from the snare.*

The colorful pile of quilts, blocks, and runners lay on the bed as my mother-in-law Priscilla showed Ellen and me one beautiful creation after another from her stash. Attracted by one of them, I reached forward to pull it from the collection. The block, in shades of brown and cream, showed a star in the background made of triangles and a set of lines creating a frame around it. "It's called Star Lane," Priscilla said, smiling. Fingering the block, she mentioned how difficult it was to make the points match up.

I recalled Priscilla's words about the tricky points and lines as I watched my son James try to balance as he walked along the logs in our Lake Easton campsite. Up and down he went as he wobbled on the downed trees. Once he slipped off, scraping his hand and knee. I noticed he always watched his feet. I stood at the end of one log and told my boy to look me in the eye. When he did, James was able to walk its length without stumbling.

We are not so different from children. How many times do we walk around studying our own feet? We may not do this literally, but perhaps internally or spiritually. When I keep my focus on myself, my head is down and my perspective is narrow. I notice only where I am walking and am painfully aware of each step as I wobble, stumble, and slip.

However, when I fix my eyes on an external point, I am able to keep my balance. What is that point? Jesus. When focused on Him, my head is lifted up and I am looking outwards. I am able to see how my footsteps align with His. Suddenly, I can see the beauty of this world and others. He provides me with clear sight, perspective, wisdom, and purpose for every step.

The balance that Christ gives helps us glide over the bumpy, narrow lanes as if they were flat, wide sidewalks. Where do we fix our eyes as we walk through life? Is it on our own feet, keeping track of each step so that we falter? Rather, Jesus invites us to look full in His face. Gazing upon Him, our confidence grows as He steadies our steps.

My Prayer

Jesus, how often do I walk along with limited vision and understanding? How many times do I slip because I am not looking at You? Help me to keep my eyes looking up. I want to walk without stumbling because You give me Your perspective on life. I want to live in the balance and grace You freely give.

My Response

My eyes are always on You, Lord.

TUMBLING BLOCKS

Deuteronomy 6:6-9—*These commandments that I give you today are to be upon your hearts. Impress them on your children. Talk about them when you sit at home and when you walk along the road, when you lie down and when you get up. Tie them as symbols on your hands and bind them on your foreheads. Write them on the doorframes of your houses and on your gates.*

I imagined my great-great-grandmother Ida and her daughter Maude sitting side by side, stitching the quilt that lay between them. It was to be a gift for my grandparents' first Christmas together in 1932. The diamond-shaped pieces lay in stacks of bright reds, yellows, blues, and greens. The ones already stitched together spilled across the quilt top. Ida and Maude smoothed it out between them, admiring their creation. The blocks tumbled all the way down the length of the quilt. When finished, they would tie each of the diamond tips with a bit of red yarn.

Al and Fern, my grandparents, treasured their gift. This Tumbling Blocks quilt graced their bed for many years until it became too fragile to use. In such bad shape that it couldn't be restored, Fern packed up the cherished gift and carefully stored it away. In 1995, Fern pulled out her quilt, pondering what to do with it. *Should it go to her only daughter? What about her boys or the grandchildren?* An idea crept into her mind: *What if she had the quilt cut apart and then framed the individual sections?* That Christmas she and Al gave the quilt pieces to all of her children and grandchildren. Each of the family now owned a piece of their North Dakota history.

Today, the Tumbling Blocks quilt section hangs on one of the walls of my home. With pride, I look at it often and think of my grandparents and my great-grandmothers. Although they are all gone, I have a thread of their past. To me, the patches they so carefully stitched represent more than just pieces of fabric from their scrap bag. They were not just shaping patterns from material, but impressing character, morals, and ideals. Ida and Maude were transferring their set of values into the hearts of the newlyweds, carefully creating a gift of love. Fern was also thinking to the next generation and wanted to leave a bit of herself for her children.

Just as Fern chose to cut her quilt apart to share it with her entire family, Jesus urges us to share ourselves with the individuals that He has placed in our lives. God yearns for His commandments to be impressed upon our hearts. They are to be part of our everyday life and should be taught to our children. Sharing the Good News of His sacrificial love is the most important gift we can pass on. Ida and Maude's precise stitches have reached across four generations. Not only have they left their impression in the quilt, but their lives also reflected a life-long faith in Jesus Christ.

My Prayer

Lord, like the splashes of color that spill across a quilt top, let Your love bring light and color to the people that You have placed in my life. Like a quilt bound together with bits of red yarn, help me tie Your commandments to my soul. I want to remember that Your life was freely broken into bits and Your blood was poured out for me. Help me to write Your words on the doorframe of my heart.

My Response

I talk about the commandments of God when I am at home or out, when I lie down or get up.

110

UNIQUE DESIGN

James 1:2-4—Consider it pure joy, my brothers and sisters, whenever you face trials of many kinds, because you know that the testing of your faith produces perseverance. Let perseverance finish its work so that you may be mature and complete, not lacking anything.

I gazed at the quilt hanging on display at the weekend quilt show. I was intrigued by its name, Unique Design. Each block cradled the four sails of a windmill. My thoughts returned to my trip to the Netherlands and the majestic working windmills I had seen. My sister Becky and I visited a mill-turned-museum one afternoon while in Leiden. The eighteenth-century wood and brick structure stood about seven stories high. We climbed the flight of tiny, ladder-like stairs to the top. As we looked down the central shaft, its enormous wheels, gears, and cogs were visible. We stepped out onto the balcony, which wound around the entire building. This area was used by farmers to access the large, wooden, slatted sails anchored to the mill. The four sails could be moved into any position to catch the breeze, harnessing its power to grind grain or pump water.

Like the farmers who employ the power of the air currents, Jesus harnesses the winds and trials of our life. Sometimes He turns us into the face of the gale and things seem to spin wildly out of control. It's natural to be afraid and want to turn away from the storm. However, when we are firmly anchored in Christ, our trials and shifting circumstances can become God's tools to help us grow. We begin to see His faithfulness to us. He has promised that He will use our troubles and hardships so that we might grow into maturity and patience.

Looking once more at the Unique Design quilt, I noticed the windmill's blades were anchored into the center of the square. Throughout the good and bad times of our lives, Jesus remains the anchor and the center of our faith. We can trust that He is using the winds and trials to teach us perseverance, which grows our faith. Like the windmill, Jesus is the source of our strength and stability and is the power behind us.

My Prayer

Jesus, it's so hard to have my life spin out control when You've placed me into the wind. Sometimes I want to turn away. But I know You will always do what's best. You want to teach me and to cause me to grow. So, please, help me accept the winds You've brought into my life. Help me hang on tightly to You because You are my strong anchor.

My Response

The testing of my faith develops perseverance. I want to be mature and complete, not lacking anything!

114

WINDING WALK

Proverbs 3:5-6—*Trust in the LORD with all your heart and lean not on your own understanding; in all your ways submit to him, and he will make your paths straight.*

Tears pricked my eyes as I leaned against the glass booth in frustration. How could I not do something as simple as make a phone call? A special token was needed, not a coin! I was finally in Brazil teaching English to young adults. I was living a dream come true and yet it challenged me on every level. During my first few weeks, I could barely understand Portuguese. Normally a calm person, I felt anxious almost all of the time. I often didn't understand what was happening—like the behavior of my students, how long we'd be staying for a visit at a neighbor's home, or where the city bus was going. I had to follow others' cues. I speak Spanish so I could pick up some meanings, but I was so dependent on my native speaker friends to explain local ways to me. I was on a winding road, not knowing where the next bend would take me. I needed God and my Brazilian friends to constantly help me. Little by little, I learned to trust God in my discomfort and sent up silent prayers throughout the day.

Helpless. Dependent. Wondering what lay ahead. Like me on my foreign travels, could this be how pioneer women felt as they walked West with their families as oxen pulled covered wagons? Could these feelings and harrowing experiences have been the inspiration for the Winding Walk quilt? One variation of the quilt block has six triangle prongs pointing in four directions. The design may have represented their vulnerability and dependence on Providence on the Oregon and California trails in the mid-1800s. By the tens of thousands, settlers gave up their homes, the support of extended family, and desire for security to move to Oregon Territory or California. Why did they risk it all? To join their loved ones in staking a claim and to yield their lives to new dreams.

Helpless. Dependent. Wondering what lay ahead. Could this be how Christ might have felt as a young boy growing up in Nazareth? The Son of God was sent to earth in the most vulnerable state. He was born in a manger to a young virgin. As a child, Jesus was utterly dependent on His parents' love, care, and guidance. As He grew to be a man of stature, wisdom, and understanding, His heart yielded to the will of His Heavenly Father.

God, in His unfathomable love for us, made His Own Son physically vulnerable and dependent. Why? Perhaps to better understand us, His wayward, fearful children. He supports us in our helplessness and walks with us through our challenges. Jesus invites us on a holy path to a new Promised Land, an abundant life yielded to Him.

My Prayer

Lord, please help me trust in You with all my heart. Help me not rely on my limited understanding of changing situations. Help me turn to You and rely on You on this winding path called Life. I know You will make my way straight if I just trust You.

My Response

As I trust in the Lord, He will make my way clear.

118

YANKEE PUZZLE

Deuteronomy 5:16—*Honor your father and your mother, as the* LORD *your God has commanded you, so that you may live long and that it may go well with you in the land the* LORD *your God is giving you.*

Driving to McDonald's one afternoon with my father, I asked him about some of the old jingles he remembered listening to on the radio when he was a boy. From seemingly out of nowhere, Dad began singing in a low, steady voice a song he learned as a Boy Scout at Camp Pomperaug, which he attended in the 1940s:

My ears are made of leather
And they flap in rainy weather
Gosh all hemlock

I'm tough as a pine nut
I'm a good old Connecticut Yankee
Can't you see?
Hey!

This spontaneous song I'd never heard revealed a side of my salt-of-the-earth, New Englander father: his boyhood memories. Recalling a few Girl Scout songs, I sang for my dad and we enjoyed sharing funny tunes. The relationship I've shared with my parents changes as we age. The times I have spent listening to my wise father have given me new insights. His memories and stories are an unfolding mystery. What I learn about my dad expands my childhood views. New understanding and compassion are added to my knowledge.

The entwined memories and character that make up my father's life are much like the scraps that create the Yankee Puzzle quilt. The hidden complexity of the quilt block, with its interlocking triangles forming diamonds, creates a subtle pattern as geometric shapes yield to other patterns. An appreciation of the quilt grows as the design is revealed. Likewise, our admiration and respect for our parents deepen as we spend time with them, listening and learning facets of their life history and personal experiences.

Just as our earthly parents may be a deep and unfolding puzzle, so our Heavenly Father is an unfathomable mystery. His thoughts are hidden from us, but the Bible gives us glimpses of His faithfulness generation after generation. Like the classic lines of the Yankee Puzzle quilt square, God's proverbs and decrees have simple yet wise truths. God asks us to honor our parents. As we do, He promises to bless us and says it will "go well" with us. As we obey His commands, He faithfully imparts His favor, protection, and provision.

My Prayer

God, thank You for my heritage. Let me honor and bless my parents. Let me see them as You see them. Thank you for the unfolding mystery of knowing You. You have been faithful and promise it will go well for me as I love and obey You.

My Response

I honor my father and my mother as the Lord has asked me.

CONTACT INFORMATION

To order additional copies of this book, please visit
www.redemption-press.com.
Also available on Amazon.com and BarnesandNoble.com
Or call toll free 1-844-2REDEEM (273-3336)